Natural Thrills

Downhill Skateboarding
and Other
EXTREME SKATEBOARDING

by Drew Lyon

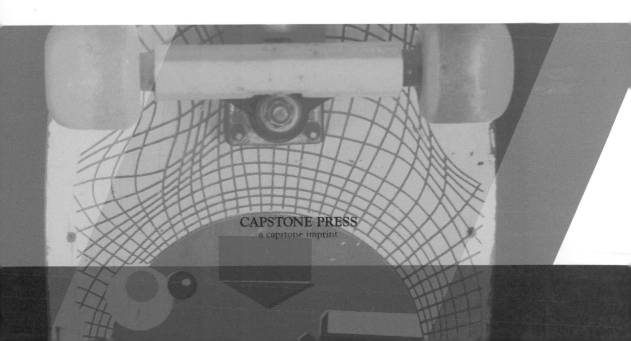

CAPSTONE PRESS
a capstone imprint

Edge Books is published by Capstone Press,
an imprint of Capstone.
1710 Roe Crest Drive
North Mankato, Minnesota 56003
www.capstonepub.com

Library of Congress Cataloging-in-Publication Data
is available on the Library of Congress website.
ISBN: 978-1-5435-9002-9 (hardcover)
ISBN: 978-1-4966-6607-9 (paperback)
ISBN: 978-1-5435-9006-7 (ebook pdf)

Editorial Credits
Anna Butzer, editor; Cynthia Della-Rovere, designer;
Kelly Garvin, media researcher; Katy LaVigne,
production specialist

Photo Credits
Alamy: H. Mark Weidman Photography, 28, Ladi Kirn, 12-13, manwithacamera.com.au, 15; Dasha Vader,
5; iStockphoto: carrotfoto, 18, dsafanda, 27, fillbuster, 21, Koke Mayayo, 24-25; Jeff Suchy Photography,
29; Maxime Lassale Photography, 6; Shutterstock: homydesign, 8, Izf, 17, Jacob Lund, cover, back cover,
Patterstock, 20, Sarah Jessup, 23, Sean Xu, 11

Artistic elements: Shutterstock: johnmarsland, pupsy

All internet sites appearing in back matter were available and accurate when this book was sent to press.

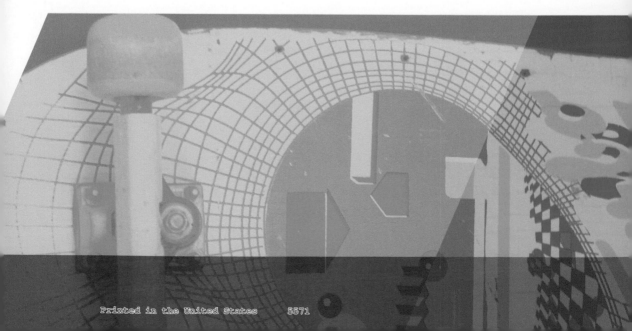

Table of Contents

CHAPTER 1

Ladies First

Downhill skateboarder Rachel "Bagels" Bruskoff rides **regular**, but she admits, "I'm definitely goofy." Bruskoff has been a professional downhill skateboarder since 2013. But don't mistake her bright smile and happy-go-lucky attitude for a relaxed approach to skateboarding. Bruskoff is a fierce competitor. She rides to win. She shouldn't be underestimated when she's **raging** down a hill. On a skateboard, Bruskoff is all business. Well, mostly. She always keeps in mind the joy skateboarding brings her.

"Some chase the glory, some chase the fun," Bruskoff says. "Skating is something that is so humble, so pure and raw, but can also be a form of competition."

Rachel Bruskoff shows her skills while controlling her speed around a corner.

Bruskoff is one of the world's most high-profile downhill skaters. She has placed second and third in worldwide rankings. She has won multiple races and achieved many **podiums** across the globe. In 2019 Bruskoff was selected to compete in the World Roller Games. She also was welcomed onto the first USA National Downhill Skate Team.

regular—the skateboarding stance in which the skater rides with their left foot forward
rage—to move quickly down a hill with intensity and speed
podium—a platform where the top three athletes receive their medals

CHAPTER 2

What Is Downhill Skateboarding?

Downhill skateboarding, also known as downhill longboarding, is a daring extreme sport. Driving in a car down a curvy road at a high speed is one matter. Zooming downhill at similar speeds on a narrow skateboard is a whole other set of wheels.

Rachel Bruskoff flies down a hill. Professional downhill skaters at Bruskoff's level travel at speeds above 50 miles per hour (80 kilometers per hour). Talk about a rush!

Downhill skateboarding became popular with the introduction of drop deck longboards in the 1970s and 1980s. Drop deck boards provided skaters greater control and a lower center of gravity.

Before mastering the sport, downhill skateboarders must first learn the basics. Core skills help an athlete learn to ride with speed while also staying safe.

Many skateboarders enjoy **carving**. An athlete keeps her knees bent while leaning forward or backward to shift weight on the board. The S-shape created when carving helps an athlete control speed while going down steep hills.

carve—to make sharp turns on a skateboard without skidding

A skateboarder places more weight on the front of the board while tucking. This helps the athlete gain speed.

Tucking is another basic skateboarding move. An athlete bends his knees while keeping his head up and chest level to the ground. Crouching low to the board helps a skateboarder pick up speed by creating less wind resistance. Many beginners find tucking an unnatural stance at first.

Cruising is ideal for beginners and casual riders. Cruisers should choose a longer board ranging between 38 to 46 inches (97 to 117 centimeters). The wheels on a cruising board should be in the 68 to 75 millimeter range.

Drafting, similar to tucking, means increasing speed while decreasing wind resistance. Being the leader of the pack isn't always a benefit. Boarders can use the person in front of them as a windbreaker. Drafting allows boarders to move faster down the hill.

Breaking the Glass Ceiling

Rachel Bruskoff's friend and competitor Emily Pross is one of the world's top downhill skaters. She's been crowned the international women's champion for three straight years. Pross bests most of her male competitors, finishing multiple years in the top 10 worldwide.

tucking—a skateboarding maneuver in which an athlete crouches low to the board in order to gain speed
cruising—a relaxed style of skateboarding that is typically used for transportation
drafting—a strategy in which an athlete closely follows another to reduce air resistance

Downhill skateboarders know better than most that it is important to reduce speed before turning a corner. **Drifting** is a common **maneuver** used to safely turn a corner. A successful drift occurs when an athlete enters a corner at a fast speed, slides to slow down, and regains traction without coming to a complete stop. Learning to drift is an important step to becoming a skilled downhill skateboarder. A racer must trust both the board and wheels while drifting.

The Need for Speed

Peter Connolly, a European downhill skateboard legend, went for the record books in 2017. At a gravity sports tournament in Quebec, Canada, Connolly was clocked at 91.17 miles per hour (146.72 kilometers per hour), a world record. Connolly lived up to his working motto: "Skate faster."

An athlete drifts around a corner to control speed.

Learning to stop is a necessary skill in downhill skateboarding. For beginners, the best and simplest way to stop on a longboard is by using a foot brake. The skater should have one stable foot in front of the board. To stop, the skater lifts up her back foot and drags it along the pavement. To maintain balance, an athlete should never brake with the front foot. Carving also helps a skater control speed, making it easier to stop safely.

drifting—a skill used to get around corners with a slower speed, without stopping

maneuver—a planned and controlled movement

Visual Glossary

crash pads
Helpful in absorbing impact in case of a fall. Crash pads can also protect against colder temperatures.

elbow pads
Elbow pads should be comfortable enough for total movement of the arms.

deck
Beginners should find a board they enjoy standing on and riding. Skateboarding is based on feel and it's important to find what feels best.

trucks
T-shaped pieces that help keep a board's wheels and bearings secure. Truck axles range from 100mm to 190mm wide. Narrower trucks are used more for racing and wider trucks are used more for cruising.

longboard
A downhill longboard can be anywhere from 28 to 46 inches (71 to 117 cm) long. A board's width can be anywhere from 8 to 11 inches (20 to 28 cm).

full-face helmet
When choosing a helmet, go on the safe side. Look for a full-face helmet that's either CE, ASTM, or CPSC certified. With helmets, style takes a backseat to safety.

knee pads
Knee pads help lessen and prevent injuries. They can also increase a boarder's confidence.

gloves
A must-have for performance and injury prevention. Gloves are used for protection and dragging over pavement.

CHAPTER 3

Taking It to the Streets

Across the world, more than 9 million people skateboard each year. Many of those skaters take the more extreme route by street skateboarding. By using public spaces and urban environments, street skaters view cities as one big skate park. Athletes should know that it isn't always legal, so be careful and knowledgable about where you are street skating.

Street skaters typically use a shortboard deck. A shortboard is the shortest skateboard. It is perfect for getting **air** and performing tricks. Shortboards are easier to flip but can be more difficult to land. Smaller boards are also lighter to carry. Street skaters often use longer boards as they become more advanced and grow taller.

The history of street skateboarding can't be written without the Birdman—Tony Hawk. Hawk won the National Skateboard Association's world championship for 12 straight years.

While non-skaters see stairs and handrails for walking, skaters see them as opportunities for jumps or tricks, such as **grinds**. Grinds are performed when an athlete slides a skateboard on the trucks or underside of the deck. Skaters also find abandoned areas with these kinds of features to create their own free street-skate sites.

air—to get all four wheels off the ground
grind—a trick performed by skating across an object on a skateboard's axles or underside of the deck

CHAPTER 4

Freestyle

The first skateboarders were freewheeling freestylers. There were few rules and even fewer limits in the early years of skateboarding. In the early 1960s, skaters started to further explore their creativity. In 1962 the clay composite wheel was invented, giving freestylers greater opportunities to strut their stuff.

Let the games begin! Freestyle skating was born. The first freestylers were rehearsed. They practiced routines and performed tricks one after another with a certain flow.

As time went on, advances in board and wheel technology made freestyle even more attractive. Lightweight decks, softer wheels, and even specific skate shoes to better grip the board all helped progress the skills of freestyle skaters.

Freestyle's beauty is in its simplicity. All a skater needs to perform an ollie is their board, a flat surface, and practice.

The 1970s and 1980s were the heyday for freestyle skateboarding. Many of the tricks performed in skateboarding's glory years are still popular today: **ollies**, 360 spins, and kickflips. Freestyle is considered **old-school** skateboarding and is not as widely practiced today. But for skaters who want to practice the roots of skateboarding, freestyling is the way to go.

ollie—a trick in which a skateboarder steps on the back of the board to make the board rise into the air
old-school—old-fashioned or traditional

CHAPTER 5

Ramping It Up

Vert skateboarding, like other skateboarding styles, was born in southern California. Creative skaters made magic skating in empty swimming pools. Riders used the upper portion of the pools to perform aerial tricks.

Vert skateboarders no longer need to find empty swimming pools to perfect a **drop-in** or an **axle stall**. Since first vert skaters started testing the limits in the 1960s, skateboarding ramps started appearing. Vert ramps are similar to half-pipes in snowboarding. The ramps have flat bottoms that transition to vertical tops. They are shaped like a giant U.

Vert skaters should be experienced in the basics of skateboarding. It is important to have protective equipment. Helmets, knee and elbow pads, and wrist guards are critical to ensure safety in vertical skateboarding. Often times, when falling down a ramp, it's best to try rolling on your knees to lessen the impact.

drop-in—skating down a half-pipe from the top
axle stall—stalling on both trucks of the skateboard; often used to balance the skater before dropping-in

Beginners will want to start at the bottom of a smaller ramp that is not crowded. To pick up speed on a half-pipe, skaters crouch and skate around the flat portion of the ramp. When entering the sloped part of a ramp or bowl, the skater straightens her legs and starts rising up. This act is called pumping.

Like most sports, skating works athletes both mentally and physically. Look out below! It can be scary when first learning to skate on vert ramps because of the steep incline. Relaxing your body and mind is the key to gaining the confidence for a drop-in.

A vert ramp is a form of a half-pipe. Mini-ramps are a less extreme version of a vert ramp.

When trying vertical jumps, skateboarders need to fully commit. Any hesitation could cause trouble or injury.

CHAPTER 6

Park and Ride

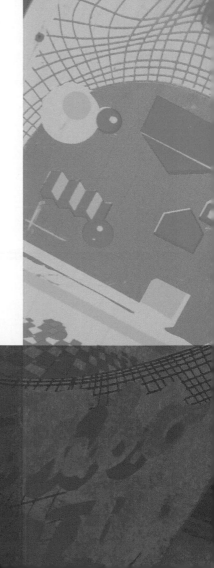

Many of the advancements in extreme skateboarding history have taken place in the western United States. The first skateboarding park, Surf City, opened in Tucson, Arizona, in 1965. The park featured concrete ramps. Surf City wasn't fancy; it didn't have the half-pipes or ramps of today's skate parks. But it was a start. By the following year, a park in Washington State opened using plywood ramps. It took 10 years before a skate park reached the United States' East Coast.

Surf City was ahead of its time. Most modern skate parks also use concrete for ramps and half-pipes because the material is cheap and low-maintenance. Skate parks are like fingerprints: no two are exactly the same. Each have their own unique designs. But most fall into three categories: bowl, street plaza, and flow parks.

Bowl parks are meant to simulate pool skating. Skaters can move around the bowl and pick up speed while keeping their feet on the board. Bowls are designed in countless shapes and designs with depths ranging from 3 to 12 feet (.91 to 3.66 meters) deep.

For those looking for the street skating experience, street plaza parks are the place to be. The design of the plaza is meant to replicate hardcore street skating, complete with benches, stairs, and railings. Plazas give skaters the best of both worlds: street skating in a safe and legal environment. Flow parks are a mix of bowl parks and plazas. The skaters pick up speed in the bowl, keeping their feet on the ground. Then they can perform tricks on street-skating objects.

A bowl park is a great place for skateboarders of all experience levels.

CHAPTER 7

Getting Started

No matter their skill level, all downhill skateboarders should use the right equipment. This starts not with the board itself but with the safety gear. Head-to-toe protective gear is a must for beginners. After picking out a board, a new skater should step on the skateboard and find out which foot feels most comfortable to lead.

An athlete's board, trucks, and wheels must be in working condition. Check the weather forecast. Rainy conditions will increase the chances of an injury. Wearing the proper protection can mean the difference between a harmless scrape and a trip to the hospital.

Being aware of your surroundings is also important. Skateboarding spills happen. Skateboarders learn to fall in ways that minimize the damage. When, where, and how you fall also matters.

Skateboarding takes bravery, commitment, and athleticism. Anyone moving more than 50 miles per hour (80 km per hour) on a set of four wheels is full of courage.

It is important to keep your eyes up when skateboarding, especially at skate parks! Collisions with other athletes are more likely to happen if you aren't aware of your surroundings.

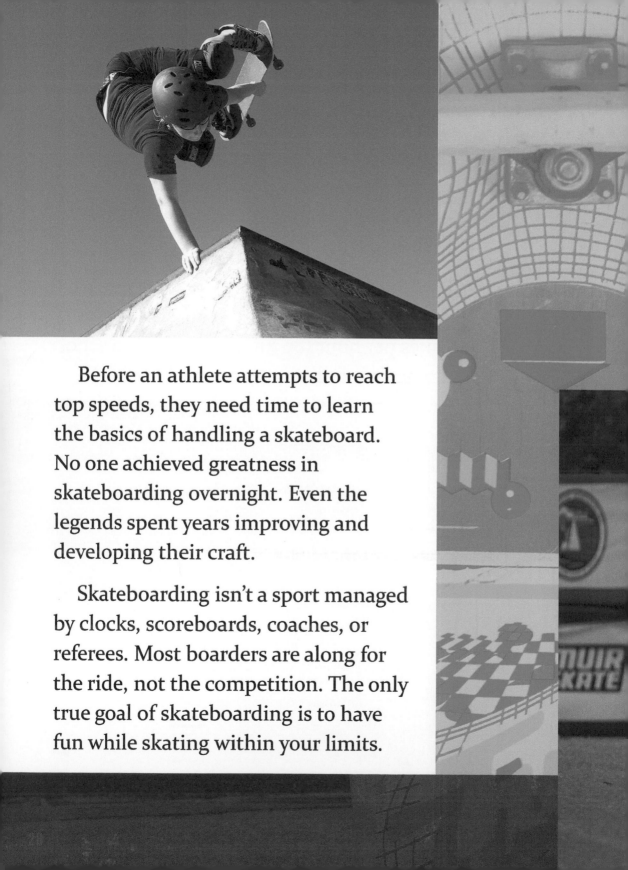

Before an athlete attempts to reach top speeds, they need time to learn the basics of handling a skateboard. No one achieved greatness in skateboarding overnight. Even the legends spent years improving and developing their craft.

Skateboarding isn't a sport managed by clocks, scoreboards, coaches, or referees. Most boarders are along for the ride, not the competition. The only true goal of skateboarding is to have fun while skating within your limits.

The skateboarding community is built around friendship and the ability to express creativity. Reaching out to a local or nearby skate park is a great first step in connecting with the skateboarding community.

Rachel Bruskoff finds her thrills on a winding, downhill road. Whether she's in her native California or the other side of the world, she never loses sight of her ultimate mission:

"Don't ever be too serious," she says. "Just have fun!"

Glossary

air (AYR)—to get all four wheels off the ground

axle stall (AK-suhl STAL)—stalling on both trucks of the skateboard; often used to balance the skater before dropping-in

carve (KARV)—to make sharp turns on a skateboard without skidding

cruising (KROOZ-ing)—a relaxed style of skateboarding that is typically used for transportation

drafting (DRAFT-ing)—a strategy in which an athlete closely follows another to reduce air resistance

drifting (DRIFT-ing)—a skill used to get around corners with a slower speed, without stopping

drop-in (DROP-in)—skating down a half-pipe from the top

grind (GRIND)—a trick performed by skating across an object on a skateboard's axles or underside of the deck

maneuver (muh-NOO-ver)—a planned and controlled movement

ollie (AH-lee)—a trick in which a skateboarder steps on the back of the board to make the board rise into the air

old-school (OLD-SKOOL)—old-fashioned or traditional

podium (POH-dee-uhm)—a platform where the top three athletes receive their medals

tucking (TUHKing-)—a skateboarding maneuver in which an athlete crouches low to the board in order to gain speed

rage (RAYJ)—to moving quickly down a hill with intensity and speed

regular (REG-yoo-lur)—the skateboarding stance in which the skater rides with their left foot forward

READ MORE

Butler, Erin K. *Extreme Land Sports*. North Mankato, MN: Capstone Press, 2018.

Enz, Tammy. *Engineering a Totally Rad Skateboard with Max Axiom*, Super Scientist. North Mankato, MN: Capstone Press, 2013.

INTERNET SITES

Concrete Disciples: Skatepark Radius Map
https://www.concretedisciples.com/index.php/skatepark-directory/usa-skateparks

Free Skateparks
http://www.freeskateparks.com/

We Are Skate Kids
http://www.weareskatekids.com

INDEX